African American History
Civil War

By Jennifer Howse

Published by Weigl Publishers Inc.
350 5th Avenue, Suite 3304, PMB 6G
New York, NY 10118-0069

Website: www.weigl.com
Copyright ©2009 WEIGL PUBLISHERS INC.

All of the Internet URLs given in the book were valid at the time of publication. However, due to the dynamic nature of the Internet, some addresses may have changed, or sites may have ceased to exist since publication. While the author and publisher regret any inconvenience this may cause readers, no responsibility for any such changes can be accepted by either the author or the publisher.

Library of Congress Cataloging-in-Publication Data available upon request.
Fax 1-866-44-WEIGL for the attention of the Publishing Records department.

ISBN 978-1-59036-876-3 (hard cover)
ISBN 978-1-59036-877-0 (soft cover)

Printed in the United States of America
1 2 3 4 5 6 7 8 9 0   12 11 10 09 08

Weigl acknowledges Getty Images as its primary image supplier for this title.

Every reasonable effort has been made to trace ownership and to obtain permission to reprint copyright material. The publishers would be pleased to have any errors or omissions brought to their attention so that they may be corrected in subsequent printings.

Editor: Heather C. Hudak
Designer: Terry Paulhus

Contents

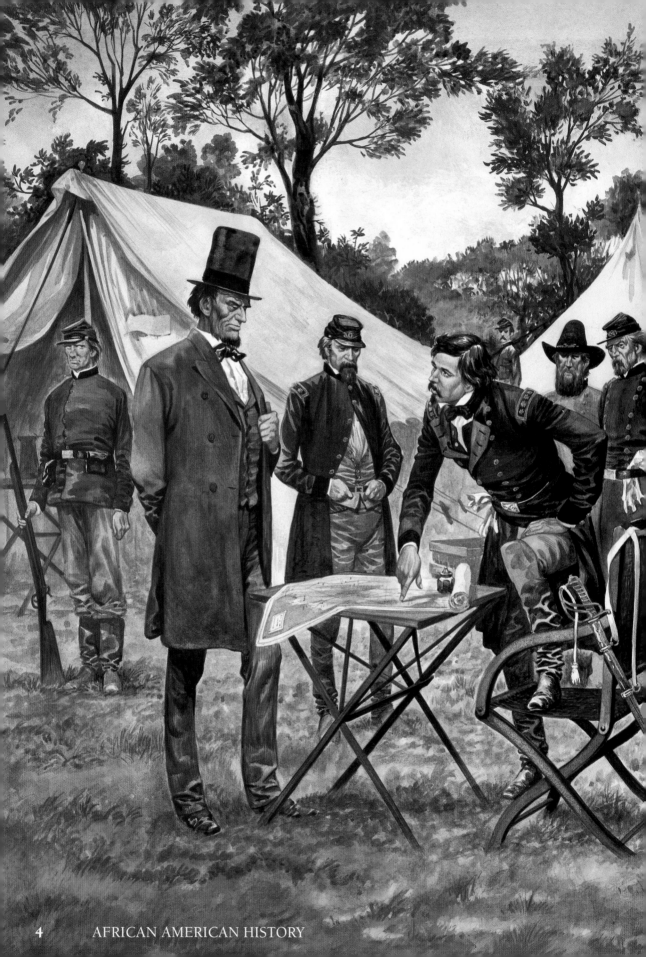

War for Freedom

Beginning in the 1600s, Africans were brought to the United States as slaves. The slaves' struggle for freedom developed into a fight for human rights and **citizenship**. Freedom and civil liberties were won in a series of political and social movements over the years. The most epic of these was the Civil War of 1861 to 1865.

In the mid-1800s, many issues divided the United States, with slavery at the forefront. Battle lines were drawn between northern **abolitionists**, who opposed slavery, and southern **confederates**, who wanted slavery to continue.

African Americans participated in the Civil War, both in the military and as slaves who were seeking their freedom. About 185,000 African Americans, made up of 163 units, served in the Union Army during the war. Both free African-Americans and runaway slaves joined the fight.

The Civil War is a part of history that forever changed the social, political, and economic patterns of the United States.

African American troops were key to the Union winning the Civil War.

TECHNOLOGY LINK

To learn more about the lives of African Americans through the words of people who lived during the Civil War, visit **http://memory.loc.gov/ ammem/snhtml/snhome.html.**

During the 1600s, 10 to 11 million Africans were forced from Africa and sent to the Americas. About 600,000 to 650,000 Africans were taken to the United States to work on farms or to do household chores.

Slave Trade in North America

In the early 1600s, European settlers began farming communities in North American colonies. Tobacco farms in Virginia required a cheap labor force. Europeans, North Americans, American Indians, and Africans were **enlisted** as **indentured workers**. After a period of working without pay, these workers could gain their freedom and own land or operate a business.

To gain their freedom, indentured workers also had to become **Christians**. However, over time, the rules changed, and any person who was not born a Christian could not gain freedom. A new race-based slavery system developed, and Africans were forced to become slaves for life. As the need for labor grew, more and more slaves were brought from Africa to North America.

Forced Journey

To acquire slaves, Africans were taken from their homeland by force. They were kidnapped, chained, and sent on a journey to the Americas. These people were forced on an overland march to slave trade forts along the coast of Africa. Then, they traveled by ship to North America. This was a period of intense hardship that lasted for two to four months. Africans were placed in small compartments on the lower decks of the ships. Each compartment was about 18 inches high and no more than 18 inches wide. During each voyage, 50 to 60 slaves out of about 500 perished of **smallpox, dysentery**, or exposure to the extreme conditions.

New Life as a Slave

Once the ships arrived in the Americas, the Africans were sold. Prodded and inspected, they were sold to the highest bidder. Families, husbands, wives, and children were separated and taken to **plantations** to begin a life of labor.

Slavery was common in the **culture** of the southern states, where farming was the main industry. These states needed huge labor forces to work on the farms, and the low cost of maintaining slaves became a common way to operate. Many of these farmers opposed paying workers because it would raise expenses and reduce profits.

Quick Facts

In the year 1619, a Dutch ship brought the first permanent African settlers to Jamestown, Virginia. The Africans worked as indentured laborers on tobacco farms.

Slavery was legalized in 1641 in the colony of Massachusetts. Soon, other colonies started allowing slavery. By 1662, Virginia had enacted a law stating that children of slaves also would be slaves.

Slave traders, the Royal African Company (RAC), transported 5,000 Africans per year between 1680 and 1686. However, the monopoly of RAC ended after a court order. As others joined in the trade, the number of slaves transported increased considerably. By the 18th century, 45,000 Africans were transported annually on British ships.

Abolitionist Movement

Enslaved African Americans fought for freedom, and groups who found slavery against their religious beliefs began to oppose slavery. The enactment of the **Bill of Rights** and the outcome of the American Revolution began to foster new ideas. Many people now believed that anyone living in the United States should have the same right to be free.

Changing the Law
Emancipation of slaves in the northern states began in the late 1700s. Great Britain outlawed the **trans-Atlantic slave trade** in 1807. Forced by slave revolt leaders, parliamentarians, and **Quakers**, the abolition of slave trade bill was passed in Great Britain, and the United States followed in 1808. Although the purchase and owning of slaves continued within the borders of the United States, Africans could no longer be legally kidnapped from their homeland.

Abolitionists
In the 1830s, efforts to abolish slavery gained momentum. Abolitionists had a common goal to free slaves, but they were divided about how slaves would live once they gained their freedom. Some wanted to help free slaves return to Africa. However, many slaves had families in the United States and did not want to leave. Others felt that a better solution would be to reform laws and help these people find new ways to live within the United States.

Amistad

In 1839, 52 members of the Mendi tribe were kidnapped from their African homeland and taken to Cuba. They were sold to slave owners and taken aboard the ship *Amistad* to another part of Cuba. After four days at sea, the Africans attacked and killed the ship's captain. They demanded that the slave owners steer the ship toward Africa. Instead, they sailed aimlessly for two months. Finally, they stopped at Long Island, New York, for food and supplies. Here, the ship was seized by authorities, and the Africans were taken into custody. Abolitionists stepped in to help the Africans with their defence. They hired lawyers, and a trial began on November 20, 1839. After evidence was presented, the trial was adjourned until January 7, 1840. Evidence supported the Africans, and the verdict was announced on January 13, 1840. The court ruled that the slaves be transported back to Africa. Although, the court case did not change the legality of slavery within the United States, it was still a victory for abolitionists. The decision enforced the law that it was illegal to kidnap Africans and bring them to the Americas.

Racism

In order to maintain the economy, supporters of slavery argued that African Americans were suited to a life of servitude and were incapable of working or living independently. These **racial stereotypes** persisted in all aspects of society.

Slavery Based Economy
In the southern states, such as Virginia, Georgia, Alabama, Louisiana, and South Carolina, economies developed rapidly with the use of slave labor. After the invention of the **cotton gin** in 1793, cotton became the main money-making crop. The cotton gin made the textile industry more profitable. African American slaves were an important part of this economy, as many worked picking cotton.

Racism as an Institution
Over time, slavery became an **institution** in U.S. society, and it was enforced by brutal laws and

Slaves were made to work at cotton gins in the late 18th century.

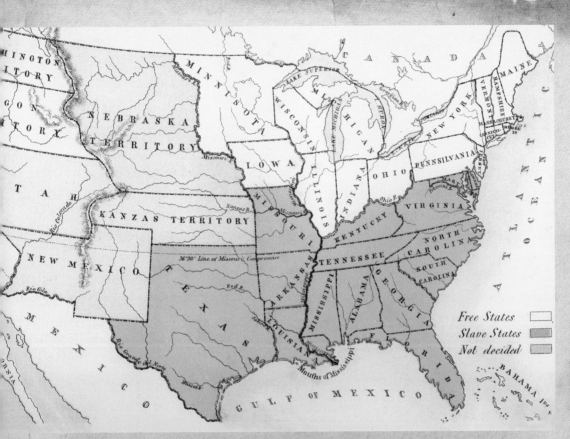

Slavery was common in many parts of the United States.

punishments. In the 19th century, the first step toward freedom for African Americans was to destroy slavery as an institution. The next step was to eliminate **racism**.

Moving Towards Freedom

All thirteen U.S. colonies had legalized slavery before the beginning of the American Revolution in 1775. By the time the United States Constitution was ratified 13 years later, five states had abolished the practice. Yet, during the 19th century, the country was divided on the issue of slavery.

The northern states abolished slavery, and African American slaves were freed. African Americans worked towards securing their rights and new-found freedom. However, African Americans still faced racism, and little progress was made as they joined the abolitionist movement.

There was division within African American communities about how to transition from a life as a slave to a free person. African Americans also struggled with ways to reduce racism so they could achieve citizenship and the right to vote.

Politics of Slavery

For politicians and lawmakers, slavery was not easily defined or changed. Although many politicians disagreed with keeping people against their will, they did not attempt to end slavery in society.

In some places, such as South Carolina, there were laws to keep the slave population under control and ensure they could not gain equality. If a slave broke these laws, there were extreme punishments, including whipping, branding, or killing. It became illegal for African Americans to gather for a funeral, to earn money, or to learn how to read and write.

Restricting Movement

In the northern free states, African Americans were required to carry a certificate that proved their freedom.

African Americans were required to carry certificates of freedom. If they did not have a certificate, they were considered fugitives. Fugitive slaves faced harsh punishments if caught running away.

Fugitive slaves who could not produce this document faced harsh punishments if they were captured. The law stated that police in free states would be fined if they did not return slaves to their owners.

A runaway slave did not have the right to representation in court. A person who helped a slave escape could face six months in prison, as well as a fine. The law attempted to discourage slaves from running away and also ensured slave owners' rights if a slave crossed state lines. This left fugitive slaves with few options or protection.

Eventually, only four states permitted African Americans to vote. However, they were still not allowed to serve on a jury or enlist in the army, despite the fact that many African Americans valiantly fought for America's freedom as part of the army led by George Washington in 1776.

Sojourner Truth

Sojourner Truth was born a slave in New York at the end of the eighteenth century. In the early 1800s, New York began passing laws to abolish slavery. However, in 1826, Sojourner escaped her life as a slave. For the next few years, she lived and worked with a Quaker family before moving to New York as a housekeeper.

In the 1840s, Sojourner began traveling across the nation to spread the word about abolition and to try to improve living conditions for African Americans. Throughout her life, Sojourner made speeches at numerous events. She is best known for the speech she presented at the Women's Rights Convention, in 1851 in Akron, Ohio. During this time, abolitionist and feminist organizations actively spread their message of freedom and equality. Men and women spoke at gatherings and openly debated with the crowd over issues such as the unfair treatment of African Americans. In her speech, Sojourner shared her experiences as an African American and also as a woman with very few civil rights. The following is an excerpt from her speech.

Sojourner Truth strongly supported civil rights for women.

"And a'n't I a woman? Look at me! Look at me! Look at my arm! (and she bared her right arm to the shoulder, showing her tremendous muscular power). I have ploughed, and planted, and gathered into barns, and no man could head me! And a'n't I a woman? I could work as much and eat as much as a man—when I could get it—and bear de lash as well! And a'n't I a woman? I have borne thirteen children, and seen 'em mos' all sold off to slavery, and when I cried out with my mother's grief, none but Jesus heard me! And a'n't I a woman?"

Life as a Slave

Historians recorded **narratives** from African Americans who lived as slaves during the 1850s and 1860s. These narratives provide an account of what day-to-day life involved for a slave in the southern United States.

Slaves began their workday at daybreak. Men and women toiled in the fields, ploughing, planting, and harvesting crops, primarily cotton. An overseer would ensure work was completed and punish slaves who did not appear to be working hard enough or performing a task correctly.

Large farms and plantations were often self-sufficient communities, where food, clothing, and housing were all manufactured by slaves. On a typical farm, the food was rationed out once a week. Most slaves lived in one-room wooden houses that had a dirt floor. They slept on beds of straw and old rags.

Slaves from two different plantations were sometimes allowed to marry. Men would visit their wives one night a week. If the

Sometimes, slaves were forced to work at gunpoint, while some were beaten if they did not carry out a task well.

A typical day for a slave started at sunrise. Slaves would till the land and run errands for their masters until sunset.

couple had children, the offspring would live with their mother.

Often, families were separated. Children would be sold to different slave owners. They were allowed to visit their mothers one day a week, or if the distance was too great, once a year. Running for freedom was common despite the fact that captured slaves were punished severely. Punishments were given out for breaking rules. Life was very difficult for slaves.

Quick Facts

In 1861, of the nine million people who lived in the southern Confederate states, 3.5 million were slaves.

An estimated 125,000 slaves had officially become freed individuals in the Confederate states as of 1861.

About 350,000 slave owners lived in the southern states. Of them, 1,800 owned more than 100 slaves.

Slave owners kept account books with the birth date, name, parent's name, and death of each slave.

Harriet Tubman

As a conductor on the Underground Railroad, Harriet Tubman took a stand against slavery. She not only risked her life to free members of her own family, but helped free many others too. The Underground Railroad was not an actual train on rails, but a route for escaped slaves to take on their journey to freedom. The route was made up of secret passages and safehouses along a path leading to the free northern states. Tubman traveled with or assisted people on their dangerous journey to the free states.

Early Beginnings

Tubman was born into slavery around 1820, on a farm in Dorchester County, Maryland. In 1849, the plantation where she lived was put up for sale, and Tubman feared that she would be sold. She waited until night fall and ran away on foot. Tubman followed the North Star and made her way to Philadelphia, where she found freedom. She came back to rescue her family.

Underground Railroad

In 1850, the Fugitive Slave Act was passed. This act stated that runaway slaves could be returned forcibly to their owner, even if they had reached a free state. At this time, Tubman decided to rescue her niece and two children from slavery. Over the next 10 years, she made 19 trips to the South and escorted more than 300 slaves along the Underground Railroad.

Inspiring Change

Tubman joined forces with Abolitionist groups and gave speeches about her activity with the Underground Railroad. After the Civil War, Tubman purchased land and a home in Auburn, New York. She joined the **women's suffrage** movement and fought for women's right to vote. In 1913, Tubman died at the age of 93.

Harriet Tubman helped many slaves find freedom.

Outbreak of War

In 1860, Abraham Lincoln was elected president of the United States. Lincoln and the **Republican party** campaigned during the election with a promise to end slavery. Some people in the southern Confederate states felt as though this was a threat to their economy.

Succession
Within three months, 11 states left the Union. They joined together in a confederacy, forming a new government under the leadership of Jefferson Davis. Lincoln tried to ease tensions with the Confederates by stating that the federal government did not intend to stop slavery or revoke the Fugitive Slave Law. However, his words did not calm the Confederates, and they only served to upset African Americans and abolitionists in the Union states. Lincoln tried to keep both sides of the dispute satisfied, but he could not make amends.

Harper's Ferry
On October 16, 1859, an abolitionist named John Brown gathered together a group of 21 African Americans and others who supported the end of slavery. He wanted to lead a war to free the slaves. The group raided the government's supply of guns and weapons at Harper's Ferry, Virginia. The attack failed, and within 36 hours, the entire group had been killed or captured. John Brown was captured. He was hanged on December 2, 1859.

This event had a big impact on the future of slavery. A group of African Americans had dared to take up arms

Abraham Lincoln angered the Confederates by promising to end slavery. This led to the formation of a new party under Jefferson Davis.

John Brown, an abolitionist, led a raid to Harper's Ferry in 1859.

against their owners. They gained the attention of many people in the Union States, and the support for the end of slavery grew.

Violent Beginnings

The Confederacy wanted to take over all government and military buildings within their newly established borders. The Union government refused to turn over military forts within the Confederacy. In protest, a Confederate army was raised, and on April 12, 1861, they attacked Fort Sumter, a federal stronghold in Charleston, South Carolina. After the battle, the Union army surrendered the fort to the Confederates. The Civil War had begun.

Quick Facts

In 1861, the Confederates held a Constitutional Convention in Montgomery, Alabama. At this convention, they created laws and rules for governing the Confederacy. The seven states agreed that Jefferson Davis would be their president, and they adopted a new constitution that gave more power to each state.

The state of Virginia was divided over the issue of joining the Confederacy. The western part of the state remained in the Union, and the eastern part seceded into the Confederacy on June 20, 1863.

The states of Delaware, Kentucky, Maryland, and Missouri remained in the Union even though they allowed slavery.

Excluded from the Fight

At the outbreak of the Civil War, free African Americans in the Union states tried to enlist in the army. They wanted to fight for the end of slavery and prove their loyalty to the Union. President Lincoln did not endorse African Americans fighting as equals in the army because he did not want to offend the Confederate states. He hoped that tensions would subside and a peaceful resolution would still be reached.

News of the War

In the Confederate states, slaves did not have access to information, and they heard about the war through their **masters**. At first, they did not understand the importance of the conflict. As the war continued, they began to realize that slavery was a big factor in the fight.

Slaveholders believed that their slaves would remain loyal and fight for their cause. Some did. However, in many cases, as slaves learned mor

Jefferson Davis, the president of the Confederate States, his cabinet and army general, used African Americans as a labor force and gave them non-military roles during the war.

about the war, they ran to Union states to help fight in the war and to seek protection from the Confederates that did not want to end slavery.

Non-Military Work

Both the Union and Confederate armies used African Americans as a labor force. They worked in non-military roles as construction laborers, cooks, horse groomers, and servants for officers. In an effort to keep up food supplies, African Americans were set to work on plantations located near military outposts. They tilled the land and grew vegetables.

Escaping to Join the Fight

It was common for slaves to attempt to escape the Confederate Army and run to the Union Army. At the beginning of the war in 1861, two slaves escaped under the cover of darkness. They paddled a canoe to the Union Army's Fortress Monroe, on the York Town Peninsula. The fortress was under the command of Brigadier General Benjamin Butler.

A Confederate officer came to the fort seeking the escaped slaves. Butler stated that the slaves would not be returned. He said that they had been taken in the same manner as equipment or weapons are taken from the enemy.

The two slaves were given paid employment with the Union Army bakery. Butler's actions were supported, and two months later, Congress passed the Act to Confiscate Property used for **Insurrectionary** Purposes. Butler's decision to keep the slaves on military grounds had led to their emancipation. Although, the confiscation law was difficult to enforce, it was part of a larger series of actions and laws that led to the emancipation of slaves.

The Emancipation Proclamation freed African American slaves and gave them many of the rights of citizenship.

Raising Armies

Sixteen months after the outbreak of war, the need for men to fight in the Union Army was growing. There were tens of thousands of casualties on both sides, and many Confederate victories created a need for more recruits.

Gaining the Right to Fight

On July 17, 1862, two Acts of Congress were passed that allowed the enlistment of African Americans into the Union Army. The first was the Militia Act and the second was the Second Confiscation Act, which freed the slaves of all disloyal owners. Owners who rebelled or were held guilty of treason with the United States were considered disloyal. Prompted by the Acts, African American men rushed to enlist, but the Act only applied to men who were free before the war started. This created a division between African American communities. To remove this imbalance, on January 1, 1863, the Emancipation Proclamation went into effect. It declared that all slaves in both Union and Confederate states would be freed on January 1, 1863. The proclamation also stated that the Union would accept all African American recruits into the Union Army.

Gathering Armies

African American abolitionists and their supporters campaigned to encourage men to join the Union Army. The Emancipation Proclamation not only freed slaves,

It gave African Americans the rights of citizenship. Abolitionists, such as Frederick Douglass, Henry Highland Garnet, and Mary Ann Shad Cary, went on recruitment drives in the North. In the South, Harriet Tubman recruited large numbers of men who were waiting for an opportunity to join the Union Army.

Unfair Treatment

African American soldiers faced poor treatment when they joined the army. They were paid $10.00 per month, compared to other recruits who received $13.00 to $21.00 per month, depending on their rank. In protest, the 54th and 55th Massachusetts Infantry refused their pay. News of this unfair treatment spread, and many African Americans refused to enlist.

On June 15, 1864, after widespread protests throughout the Union Army, African American soldiers received equal pay. However, African American soldiers still received substandard supplies and food rations.

Although, the Emancipation Proclamation had freed slaves, the official policies of segregation remained in place. Despite this, many abolitionists continued recruiting men for the military. They hoped that, if African Americans could prove themselves on the battlefield, they could earn equal rights.

Quick Facts

Enlisted African American soldiers received basic training, but this was often not enough for combat. They had inferior firearms and equipment, and poor camp conditions and hospital facilities.

The number of African Americans who enlisted in Union Army was larger than the number of soldiers in the entire Confederate Army in the final months of the war.

Posters were issued calling for African Americans to enlist in the army.

Army and Navy

African American recruits were placed in the newly formed United States Colored Troops (USCT). Only African Americans belonged to these units. In order for the government to manage these new regiments, they created the Bureau of Colored Troops. This department recruited African Americans to the army and ensured the regiments received training before heading into battle.

Army

Some African American recruits worked in infantry as foot soldiers

Illustrated posters of the Black Union Regiment were used to inspire more African Americans to enlist in the army.

and **cavalry**. Others worked in light and heavy artillery units operating big guns or canons. In total, 180,000 free African Americans and freed slaves served in 163 units during the last two years of the war. They accounted for about one-tenth of all of troops who fought in the Civil War.

Navy

Since the inception of the United States Navy and during the period in the 19th century before 1861, African Americans had been working aboard naval vessels. Free African American sailors were accepted into the United States Navy at the beginning of the war, and after 1861, former slaves were also accepted. About 18,000 men and more than a dozen women served in the navy during the war. They made up about 15 percent of the total of the enlisted force. Ship records show that African Americans served aboard almost all of the 700 vessels in the navy.

Ranks

Naval recruits were stationed without segregation aboard ships. They were granted ranks from ordinary seamen to officers.

African American recruits entered USCT army regiments with the rank of private. Advancement through the ranks was limited, but some African American soldiers were promoted to low-ranking officer status.

The first African American to receive a Regular Army Commission was Martin Robinson Delany. The Regular Commissions are permanent ranks. This meant he maintained the rank or remained a major during peacetime too, which is not the case if a person is part of a reserve of national guard. In 1865, Delany obtained the rank of major. He became a well-known military man and author.

To Serve and Protect

The Union army recruiting posters promised fugitive African Americans protection from harsh treatment by the Confederate Army.

The words of Charles Sumner, an anti-slavery leader in the Senate, were used on recruitment posters. He said that, in exchange for protection, African Americans should serve in the war.

The words were meant to encourage African American communities to fight against their enemies, the slave owners in the southern Confederate states. Recruiters hoped to attract young men by inspiring them to believe this was their fight. They wanted African Americans to believe that, if they helped in the war, other Americans would be thankful for their support and treat them with more respect.

The African American soldiers of the Union Army fought valiantly in every combat in which they took part.

Fighting the War for Freedom

African American soldiers and sailors served in many important battles during the Civil War. In the army, however, the United States Colored Troops units were not treated fairly. Many of the troops in these units were untrained because African Americans had not taken part in battles before. As a result, African Americans were not used in combat.

This changed in October 1862. African American soldiers of the 1st Kansas Colored Volunteers were given an opportunity to prove that they could take part in combat. They helped drive the attacking Confederates back at the Battle of Island Mound, Missouri.

After this, USCT units slowly started to gain the acceptance of other soldiers. By August 1863, 14 USCT Regiments had completed training and were ready for service.

Milliken's Bend

On June 7, 1863, at Milliken's Bend, Louisiana, the USCT unit and the 23rd Iowa Volunteer Infantry forced the Confederate calvary to retreat. This was the first large-scale combat engagement where the USCT played an important part in the Union Army's war efforts.

Fort Wagner

On July 11, 1863, the Union Army made a failed attempt to take over a battery fort in Charleston, South Carolina. Another assault was planned for July 18, 1863. One of the first African American units, the 54th Massachusetts Volunteer Infantry, led the assault on the strongly fortified Confederate positions. The soldiers of the 54th scaled the Confederate fortifications but were driven back after brutal hand-to-hand combat. The attack failed, but 16 African American soldiers were given the Medal of Honor for their bravery in the battle.

Fort Pillow

USCT soldiers were often victims of war crimes. These crimes included murder, ill-treatment, deportation of civilian residents, and the bombing of schools among other things. Many such crimes were directed towards African Americans during the Civil War. African Americans were not taken as Prisoners of War (POW) but were killed instead. One of the worst cases occurred at Fort Pillow, Tennessee, on April 12, 1864. After a fierce battle, the Confederate Army won control of the fort from Union soldiers. The Confederates demanded the surrender of the 550 Union Army soldiers, about half of which were African American. At the time, upon surrender, troops were to be treated as POWs. However, it is believed that African American soldiers were shot to death instead. Only 62 of these soldiers survived.

Many USCT troops were brutally killed at the Fort Pillow combat because of their race. Soldiers of European ancestry were taken as prisoners of war.

TECHNOLOGY LINK
For an overview of the Civil War, including African-American histories, visit **www.itd.nps.gov/cwss/ history/aa_history.htm**.

Life as a Soldier

Very few African Americans could read or write at the beginning of the war. Some of those who could kept diaries and journals about their experiences. William Benjamin Gould was one of the only African Americans to keep a diary. Gould's diary begins by explaining how he was a slave who escaped from Wilmington, North Carolina, to join the Union Navy. It also tells of his day to day activities as a sailor.

Many African Americans from the southern Confederate states had similar stories of escape to the Union forces. Albert Jones, a born slave, left

African American soldiers often catered to officers of European ancestry.

his master's home when he was 21 years of age. After having a series of adventures to avoid re-capture, he joined a crew that was working to replace a bridge that had been torn down by retreating Confederate troops. Jones was recruited from the crew and enlisted into the USCT cavalry. His diaries explain how he served for three-and-a-half years as one of the first African American cavalry troops.

Many African Americans also served in the Confederate army. Frank Range, another slave, was taken into the military service by his master, Jim Herbert. Range worked as a cook, but he also was pressed into combat. In his diary, Range recalls how he worked alongside Confederate soldiers as they built barriers to slow the advance of the Union forces. They would dig a ditch and cover it over with trees to hide beneath. During one bombardment of their lines at Richmond, Virginia, the barrier fell on Range's master, Jim Herbert. Range pulled Herbert out to safety. However, this act of bravery and loyalty did not win a mention in the history of African American slaves who stood by their masters.

Combat Honors

Battle honors were given to African Americans in both the army and navy. Twenty-five African American soldiers were awarded the Congressional Medal of Honor. Fourteen of these were given to African American soldiers who had taken part in the Battle of Chaffin's Farm Virginia. Another four received the award after the Battle of Mobile Bay.

Created in 1861, the Congressional Medal of Honor is the most prized award a person serving in the U.S. armed forces can receive for bravery in times of battle.

To be considered for this award, a person must have committed an act of bravery that put his own life at risk in an effort to save the lives of others.

More than 1,520 were given out during the Civil War, as it was the only award of its kind at that time. Today, this special medal is given out rarely. To date, Congress has awarded only 3,400 Medals of Honor.

War is Over

The last battle of the Civil War was the fall of Richmond on April 2, 1865. The city was destroyed by fires and rioting. By April 9, the Civil War was over.

In the end, about 180,000 African American soldiers had served in the Union Army. They made up about 10 percent of the entire force. Losses among African Americans were high—about one-third of those who enrolled in the military lost their lives during the Civil War.

The navy also had about 800 African American casualties. This was about one-third of the total losses. Crewmen lost, injured, or wounded in action served aboard 49 naval vessels. Another 2,000 African American seamen died of disease. Several USCT regiments

The first and only president of the Confederate States, Jefferson Davies, left Richmond after it was destroyed by fires and rioting in the last battle of the Civil War in 1865.

were kept in service until 1867. They were part of the occupation forces in the former Confederate states. These forces helped maintain the peace and curb lawlessness in the southern states. These men also helped with the reconstruction of cities and towns that had been destroyed by the war.

Veterans of the USCT faced many struggles after the war. African Americans were not thought to be familiar with political, economical, social, or environmental issues of the state. As a result, they were not considered concerned citizens until 1890. For this reason, they did not receive the pensions that were due to them. Only in 1900 did pensions

Buffalo soldiers participated in the Indian Wars and fought in more than 177 combat engagements.

Buffalo Soldiers

Six units were established under an 1866 law that authorized the formation of an African American infantry. These were the first African American regiments in the United States Army to serve during peacetime. Soldiers serving in these units were former slaves, USCT veterans, Confederate veterans, and trained freedmen. They became known as the Buffalo Soldiers.

The name Buffalo Soldiers was given to the regiment by Cherokee Indians. The Cherokee saw two similarities between African Americans and the buffalo. Both were able to survive the harsh climates of the western states, and they had strong skills as fighters.

During the period of intense migration and settlement following the war, the Buffalo Soldiers escorted settlers, cattle herds, and railway crews to ensure their safety.

Aftermath

The Civil War was a chance for African Americans to improve their lives. A new chapter had begun with the abolishment of slavery. Four million people who were once slaves were now free. They could join together with family members, separated by the bonds of slavery or the chaos of war. Free African Americans could start a new life, working in a different career and living any place they chose.

African American slaves who were free after the Civil War looked forward to an improved life and hoped for policies that would give them rights as U.S. citizens.

However, for many, their new, free life was overwhelming after living for generations without power or control over their lives. Most slaves were set free with no place to live and no money.

After the war, African Americans faced new challenges. Securing the rights of citizenship became a focus for many.

Former slaves hoped for a new South that would embrace democratic policies that made all citizens equal. At the 1868 South Carolina Constitutional Convention, 60 of the 125 delegates were former slaves. They passed laws for public school systems, roads, health care, and women's rights. The convention offered hope that people could live in a diverse society with equal rights.

Still, these sweeping changes were opposed by many people in South Carolina who could not accept former slaves voting or being equal under the law. The election of 1873 removed most of the former slave delegates from office and ended Reconstruction in the former Confederate States. Reconstruction refers to the era when the United States government focused on resolving the consequences and aftermath of the Civil War. After a 250 year legacy of slavery, it proved difficult to change the way people thought about one another.

African Americans were elected to legislature during the 1868 election. However, the election of 1873 removed former slave delegates from office.

Quick Facts

Following the Civil War, control over the economy shifted from slave owners to large institutions and corporations, such as the federal government and railways.

Many African American soldiers used the last name of their slave master as their own when they enlisted in the military. After being freed from slavery, they changed their last names. For this reason, many records of African American in the war are inaccurate. This caused problems in later years when they applied for their pensions.

Gradual Emancipation

After the Civil War, the economy of the states had to be rebuilt, as did cities and transportation systems. The United States Constitution also had to be rewritten to include the rights of African Americans. Although freedom was won and stated in the Emancipation Proclamation, there were still many inequalities under the law after the war.

Citizenship

Abolitionists did not abandon their cause at the end of the war. They continued to lobby the government for adjustments to the Constitution to include African American rights. These adjustments were the Reconstruction era's primary **mission**. Two amendments were added to the Constitution. The Fourteenth Amendment, passed in June 1866, granted citizenship to all people born or **naturalized** in the United States. This meant that African Americans would now be considered citizens of the United States. This period of Reconstruction lasted for about 10 years.

The Right to Vote

Voting as a citizen was vital to the cause of abolitionists, who believed

The Reconstruction Era's main aim was to make adjustments to the Constitution to include African American rights. For example, African Americans could now sit on a jury during courtroom trials.

the right to vote was a key element of freedom. Veterans of USCT believed they had been promised this right when they were recruited and felt they had earned it through their military service.

In June 1865, an African American army chaplain, Garland White, wrote a letter to the editor of the *Christian Recorder*. In this letter, he asked the country to give African Americans equal rights so that they could avoid being **disenfranchised**. African Americans would be denied their legal right to vote in many states until 100 years later, when the Voting Rights Act of 1965 was passed.

Civil Rights
Unfair treatment toward African Americans persisted in many areas.

In the former Confederate states, "Black Codes" were enacted. The gains of Reconstruction faded in the face of these restrictive laws that dictated the type of jobs African Americans could have.

African Americans had to work in **agricultural** occupations and **domestic service**. In some places, they had to apply to the justice of the peace to work in a job other than agriculture. Self-sufficiency, such as growing market crops they could sell, was also discouraged. The ability to move freely and live in any place they chose was limited under the Black Codes. African Americans were barred from living in cities and towns, and visits to these places were monitored by lawmakers. The Black Codes were lifted in 1866 and were replaced by new laws.

Jim Crow

In 1877, the "Jim Crow Laws" were established as another form of political control over African Americans. These laws discouraged African Americans from settling in certain states.

Segregation was a key part of the Jim

The Jim Crow laws put an emphasis on segregation in public places, such as theaters, restaurants, and washrooms.

Crow Laws. African Americans were restricted in the ways they could use public facilities, such as schools, churches, public transportation, and even water fountains. Separate facilities were made for people of European ancestry. African Americans were not allowed to use these spaces.

Education

The Freedman's Village near Arlington was one of the many endeavors of the relief organizations created by abolitionists.

Many African Americans believed that education was key to freedom, and for some, the war provided an opportunity to get more education.

During the Civil War, African American recruits were given the opportunity to learn how to read and write. Abolitionist groups created relief organizations, such as the National Freedman's Relief Association, to provide food, clothing, and education to newly freed African Americans. Over time, education for African Americans reached all areas occupied by Union troops.

Fourteen African American chaplains served with the Union Army. They were important in educating African Americans. During the war, they helped teachers safely reach the troops. Chaplains also held reading classes.

Although only eight African American surgeons served in the Union Army, they paved the way for other African Americans to seek an education. Lieutenant Colonel Alexander Augusta was a physician who trained in Canada. After the war, he lived in Washington, DC, where he was on the board of directors for the Howard University Medical School.

The Freedman's Bureau was created in 1865 to help with education, employment, and making the transition from slave to free person. Despite the bureau's success, it was unable to cure all problems. Due to many factors, such as a lack of money, inefficiency, and corruption, the organization's efforts came to an end in 1870.

Despite the lack of government support many African Americans continued to fight for the right to education.

African American History

Historian William E. Du Bois wanted to ensure the histories of African American slaves, abolitionists, and veterans of the Civil War were not lost. Born in 1868 in Great Barrington, Massachusetts, Du Bois became a correspondent for the New York Globe at the age of 15. He was keenly aware of the importance of recording events with an African American perspective.

Du Bois completed his master's degree in the spring of 1891, and with a grant from the government, he attended the University of Berlin in Germany. During the two years Du Bois spent in Berlin, he began to see the race issues in the Americas, Africa, and Asia and Europe as one, as he united his studies of history, economics and politics into a scientific approach of social research.

Du Bois taught at various universities and researched race relations. He believed that providing knowledge to others about different cultures would help end **prejudice**.

Du Bois published more than 25 books on African American history. On August 27, 1963, on the eve of the Civil Rights March on

Washington, Du Bois died in Accra, Ghana.

Frederick Douglass

Frederick Douglass was a leader who urged all people in the United States to recognize slavery as **immoral**. He believed that freedom was a natural right for all people. Douglass was an influential speaker and author who was central in directing the abolitionist movement.

Early Beginnings

Born into slavery in 1817, Frederick Douglass grew up away from his mother and was raised by his grandmother near Holmes Hill Farm in Maryland. At the age of six, he was taken to a plantation and joined the ranks of other slave children. Douglass discovered that learning to read might help him find freedom. He gave the bread his master gave him to children of European ancestry, and in return, they taught him all they had learned in school. Douglass also picked up many words from people around him. This later came to be known as his mode of self-education.

At the age of 16, Douglass started an illegal school for slaves. Slaves would meet in secret on Sundays. During these meetings, they planned their escape from slavery. The plan was discovered, and Douglass and his group were jailed.

Upon his release, Douglass repaired boats until he saw his chance for freedom. One day, he dressed in a

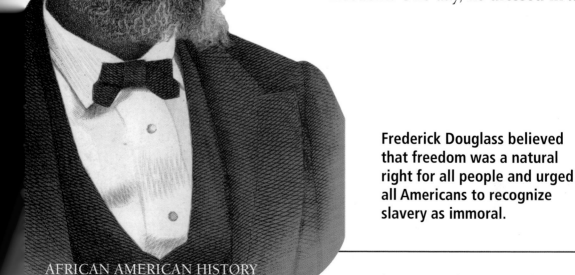

Frederick Douglass believed that freedom was a natural right for all people and urged all Americans to recognize slavery as immoral.

sailor's uniform and fled to New York City. On September 4, 1838, Douglass became a free man.

The Mission

In 1841, Douglass was asked to share his slave experiences at a meeting of the American Anti-slavery Society. This was the beginning of his career as an abolitionist. By May, 1845, Douglass had published his autobiography *Narrative of the Life of Frederick Douglass*. He toured the nation, speaking to others about his experiences.

Inspiring Change

Douglass joined the recruitment drive to enlist African American troops for the Union Army. Initially, he believed non-violent solutions to anti-slavery measures were the best approach. However, he supported Abraham Lincoln's Republican government and its hard-line stand against the Confederates. Douglass believed that African Americans needed to take part in the Union's anti-slavery movement so that they could have a voice in the new society to be formed after the abolition of slavery.

The North Star

Frederick Douglass subscribed to the abolitionist newspaper *The Liberator*, which was a weekly published by W. L. Garrison, another abolitionist. Both Garrison and Douglass were appreciative of each other, and after meeting with Douglass, Garrison mentioned the man in his weekly paper. Douglass later used his knowledge and ideas on abolition in his own weekly paper, *The North Star*, a paper dedicated to the abolition movement and improved living conditions for African Americans.

Gaining in readership, *The North Star* was circulated across the United States.

The newspaper was a forum to discuss political actions necessary to abolish slavery. *The North Star* became the *Frederick Douglass Paper* in 1951, and it continues to be published today.

A New Hope

Many African Americans led abolitionist movements that inspired generations to continue in their quest for civil rights. In 1850, it was difficult for Americans to imagine the United States without slavery. However, abolitionists fought for freedom, and they were rewarded. This fight for African American rights continued through the next century, as people sought equality for all U.S. citizens. By the 1950s, African Americans were ready to take peaceful actions to secure their rights.

Leading Change

For the first time, the "black laws" that were created at the turn of the 19th century were challenged during the civil rights protests of the 1950s and 1960s. The first major protest took place when Rosa Parks refused to give up her seat on a bus to a

The fight for equality between African Americans and people of European ancestry continued into the later part of the 20th century. Many African Americans marched to Washington to oppose segregation and support equal rights.

person of European ancestry. African American civil rights protesters and their supporters marched to back up her actions. They asked for fair and equal treatment under the law. Their voices were heard and another era began for African Americans.

The Fight for Change Continues

Through the 1980s, 1990s, and 2000s, many African Americans continued to work toward equality for all U.S. citizens. Today, African Americans serve in all areas of the United States military and within all ranks.

Movies, such as *Glory*, *The Color Purple*, and the television miniseries *Roots*, remind people today of the struggles African Americans have faced throughout U.S. history. The producers and actors in these features broke down barriers as they presented stories that demonstrated how African Americans fought to gain their freedom.

A huge crowd of African Americans came together to show their support for equal rights in the United States during the March on Washington.

TECHNOLOGY LINK

To learn more about African Americans in the Civil War, visit **www.afroamcivilwar.org**.

Timeline

1619: Africans are captured and brought to Jamestown, Virginia, to work as slaves.

1619

1807: Congress declares it illegal to bring slaves into the United States.

1831 to 1861: About 75,000 slaves escape by the Underground Railroad, a network that helped protect and hide escaped slaves so they could find freedom.

1861: The Civil War begins. One of the main issues behind the conflict is to determine if slavery should be allowed.

1863: President Abraham Lincoln passes the Emancipation Proclamation, which legally frees all slaves.

1865: Congress passes the Thirteenth Amendment, which outlaws slavery.

1866: Congress passes the Civil Rights Act, which declares African Americans citizens.

1881: The first Jim Crow law is passed in Tennessee.

1896: In Plessy v. Ferguson, the Supreme Court rules that public places may be segregated as long as equal facilities are given to African Americans.

1909: The National Association for the Advancement of Colored People (NAACP) is formed.

1910-1920: During a period known as the Great Migration, about 500,000 African Americans move to northern states.

1861

1914: Marcus Garvey forms the Universal Negro Improvement Association in Jamaica. The group eventually opens branches in the United States.

1919: A series of violent events occur in response to the Great Migration. The period is known as "Red Summer" because of the hundreds of deaths that resulted from the violence.

1909

1600   **1800**   **1850**   **1900**

1942: The Congress of Racial Equality (CORE) is started in Chicago.

1948: President Truman desegregates the army.

1954: In Brown v. Board of Education of Topeka, the Supreme Court rules against school segregation.

1955: The Montgomery Bus Boycott begins when Rosa Parks refuses to give up her seat to a passenger of European ancestry.

1957: A community in Little Rock, Arkansas opposes desegregation, and plans a protest to prevent nine African American students from entering a school that was formerly only for students of European ancestry. The African American students are later called "The Little Rock Nine."

1960: At a Woolworth's lunch counter in Greensboro, North Carolina, four African American college students hold the first sit-in.

1961: The Congress of Racial Equality (CORE) begins to organize Freedom Rides.

1963

1963: Martin Luther King, Jr. writes "Letter from a Birmingham Jail."

1964: Martin Luther King, Jr. is awarded the Nobel Peace Prize.

1965: Malcolm X is assassinated in New York.

1983: Astronaut Guion "Guy" S. Bluford, Jr., becomes the first African American in space, flying aboard the space shuttle *Challenger*.

1985: Philadelphia State Police bomb a house in Philadelphia occupied by an African American activist organization, MOVE, killing 11 occupants and triggering a fire that destroys a neighborhood and leaves more than 300 people homeless.

1986: Martin Luther King, Jr.'s birthday is made into a national holiday.

1989: General Colin L. Powell is the first African American to be named chair of the Joint Chiefs of Staff of the U.S. military.

1989: Oprah Winfrey becomes the first African American woman to host a nationally syndicated talk show.

2008: Barack Obama, a politician from Chicago's South Side, becomes the first African American to secure a major party nomination as a presidential candidate.

1961

2008

1950   1960   1980   2000

Activity

Become A Historian

History is the written record of the lives of people who have lived in the past. Historians research these records and share their findings with others so everyone is enriched by the experiences of people and events that have shaped the world.

Think about an event in the past 25 years that you would like to know more about. This can be a major event in the world, or it may be something that happened in the place where you live. Write down six questions about this time. You may want to know what it was like to live at this time or how the event changed the way people lived.

You will need:

✓ pen
✓ paper

Find a person who lived during this time that you can interview about the event. Begin by recording your name, the date of the interview, the name and birth date of the person you are interviewing, as well as any other important information, such as the names of his or her spouse and children. Then, ask the six questions you wrote down earlier. Record the responses. Be sure to accurately quote every word.

You have created an historic record. Consider the answers you received to your questions. Does the information you gathered cause you to view this event differently? What new things did you learn?

Test Your Knowledge

Q Why did the 54th Massachusetts refuse to accept their pay?

A They were protesting unequal pay.

Q On which railway was Harriet Tubman a conductor?

A The Underground Railroad

Q How many African Americans were awarded the Congressional Medal of Honor for service during the Civil War?

A 25

Q What was the name of Frederick Douglass's self-published newspaper?

A The North Star

What is the nickname of the first African American regiment to serve during peacetime?

A Buffalo Soldiers

Q What was the first set of restrictive laws called that reduced the civil rights of African Americans during the 1860s?

A The Black Codes

Further Research

Books

Learn more about slavery and the Civil War by reading the following books.

Dean Myers, Walter. *Now Is Your Time: The African-American Struggle for Freedom*. New York: HarperCollins Children's Books, 1992.

Gorrell, Gena K. *North Star to Freedom: the Story of the Underground Railway*. New York: Delacorte Press, 1997.

Websites

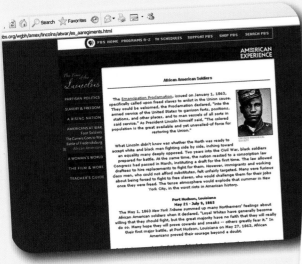

To learn more about African American Civil War soldiers, visit **www.pbs.org/wgbh/amex/lincolns/ atwar/es_aaregiments.html**.

Find out more about the events and the people of the Civil War at **http://lcweb2.loc.gov/ammem/ ndlpedu/features/timeline/civil war/aasoldrs/soldiers.html**.

Glossary

abolitionists: people who are against slavery

agricultural: food and textile production

Bill of Rights: the list of rights for citizens

cavalry: the part of a military force composed of troops that serve on horseback

Christians: people who belong to religious sects that started in Middle East and Europe

citizenship: the criteria for belonging to a nation

Confederates: supporters of the Confederate States of America

cotton gin: a machine that separates sticky green cotton seeds from the cotton boll

culture: the way people live together

disenfranchised: being deprived of the rights of citizenship, including the right to vote

domestic service: work that is part of maintaining a household

dysentery: an infection of the intestines marked by severe diarrhea

emancipation: freeing someone from the control of another

enlisted: military recruits who signed themselves up for service

fugitive: a person running from authority

immoral: violating moral principles of personal and social ethics.

indentured workers: working under a contract

institution: an official and accepted authority

insurrectionary: a gathering of people to overthrow authority

masters: what the owners of slaves called themselves

master's degree: an advanced degree

mission: the purpose and intent of a person or organization

narratives: written personal stories of life experiences

naturalized: a person who has lived within a country long enough to be a considered a citizen

plantations: large scale farming operations

prejudice: beliefs that restrict a specific group

Quakers: a popular name for a members of the Religious Society of Friends

racials stereotypes: beliefs that a person's race determines who and what they are

racism: judgments about people based on their race

Republican party: One of the parties in the United States two-party system

smallpox: a type of serious infectious disease in which there is a severe rash of large, pus-filled spots that usually leave scars

trans-Atlantic slave trade: economy of kidnapped Africans, shipped and sold in the Americas

women's suffrage: women's movement to gain the right of citizenship and voting

Index